K-OFF!

All these footy heroes, plus loads more, star in your awesome annual!

MATCH OF THE DAY ANNUAL

D0236742

WAYNE ROONEY
MAN. UNITED
2010 MEGA MOMENT...
SCORING FOUR GOALS IN ONE GAME AGAINST HULL!

STEVEN GERRARD
LIVERPOOL
2010 MEGA MOMENT...
SAYING HE WON'T LEAVE LIVERPOOL!

ROBIN VAN PERSIE
ARSENAL
2010 MEGA MOMENT...
SCORING TWO GOALS AS HOLLAND REACHED THE WORLD CUP FINAL!

CRISTIANO RONALDO
REAL MADRID
2010 MEGA MOMENT...
SCORING 26 GOALS IN JUST 29 GAMES!

ANNUAL SPECIAL! GOSSIP!

HOTTEST RUMOUR 2011

Everybody wants a piece of me!

TORRES TO CHELSEA?

We've got some bad news for **Liverpool** fans thinking the Roy Hodgson revolution is well under way – in fact, it's very bad news. Superstar striker **Fernando Torres** may have committed his future to the club last summer, but we hear **Chelsea** will return in the New Year with a mega bid of £50 million. The Reds would struggle to turn that down!

HOW TORRES COULD LOOK AT CHELSEA!

SURPRISE STAR OF THE YEAR!

PAUL THE OCTOPUS One minute, he's slobbing about in a fish tank, the next, he's a global phenomenon!

STUPID INJURY OF THE YEAR!

JAMIE LANGFIELD Aberdeen's keeper was out for weeks after spilling hot water on his foot – while making tea!

WORST HEADER OF THE YEAR!

Ooof!

ASHLEY COLE Proof that even the world's best players can mess up. Keep your eyes open next time, Ash!

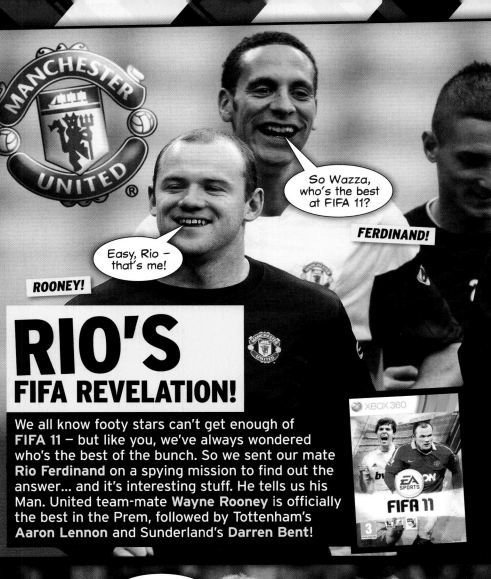

So Wazza, who's the best at FIFA 11?

FERDINAND!

Easy, Rio – that's me!

ROONEY!

RIO'S
FIFA REVELATION!

We all know footy stars can't get enough of **FIFA 11** – but like you, we've always wondered who's the best of the bunch. So we sent our mate **Rio Ferdinand** on a spying mission to find out the answer... and it's interesting stuff. He tells us his Man. United team-mate **Wayne Rooney** is officially the best in the Prem, followed by Tottenham's **Aaron Lennon** and Sunderland's **Darren Bent**!

XBOX 360
EA SPORTS
FIFA 11
3

You are my *Tweet*-heart, Ashley!

MESSI!

F C B

MESSI'S
YOUNG LOVE!

Who does **Lionel Messi** spend his Saturdays drooling over on TV? Aston Villa star **Ashley Young**, that's who! He watches the Prem on telly and says he loves the Villa winger. Messi even wrote on Twitter earlier this year: "The Villa v West Ham match is really exciting – Ashley Young is having a blinder!"

Thanks for watching!

YOUNG!

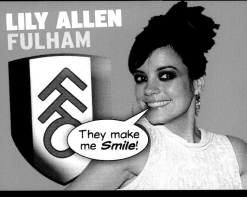

FOOTY FUNNIES!

PART ONE!

FOOTBALLERS DO THE FUNNIEST THINGS...

Who are you calling a bighead?

JAPAN KEEPER FALLS ASLEEP AND MISSES BALL GOING IN...

Zzzzzzzzzzzz...

What the chuff is that?

Make it go away!

I'll call a doctor!

Laugh if you fancy Susan Boyle!

Ha-ha! Not me nipples!

EVERTON STARS AMAZED BY CAPTAIN'S ARMBAND...

JAASKELAINEN FINDS PAUL ROBINSON'S TICKLISH SPOT...

MAN. CITY'S £1 BILLION MAKEOVER!

MOTD reveals how Man. City's mega-rich owner took his spending past £1 billion in 2010!

M.C.F.C.

Superbia In Praelio ™

£350 MILLION ON PLAYERS!

Something tells us that City owner Sheikh Mansour thinks that he's playing Footall Manager 2011 – that's because he uses the same transfer strategy in real life as we do in the computer game! If another club tries to buy the player you want, offer a few more million – and he's all yours!

MILNER!
£24 million

TEVEZ!
£47.5 million

SILVA!
£24 million

YAYA TOURE!
£24 million

TOTAL SPEND: £1.07 BILLION!

£20 MILLION ON NEW FACILITIES!

Sir Alex Ferguson isn't joking when he calls City "noisy neighbours" – they've had the builders in revamping their training ground, which is just down the road from Man. United's!

£210 MILLION TO BUY THE CLUB!

The spending began back in 2008, when Sheikh Mansour found enough spare change down the back of his sofa to buy Man. City for £210 million!

THE SHEIKH!

£487.8 MILLION ON WAGES!

Can you believe that new midfield star Yaya Toure is rumoured to be earning £220,000 every week at Man. City? The club has now paid out nearly £500 million in wages and fees since 2008!

WHAT THEY COULD'VE GOT FOR THAT MONEY...

2.6 million iPHONES!

7701 MONSTER TRUCKS!

4.3 million PAIRS OF WAYNE ROONEY'S BOOTS!

LIONEL MESSI

BARCELONA & ARGENTINA

PLAYER PROFILE

POSITION: Forward
AGE: 23
VALUE: £100 million
DID YOU KNOW?
Messi was crowned
World and European
Player of the Year
in 2009!

MATCH OF THE DAY

WORLD STAR!

TOP 10 201

MOTD looks back at the Top 10 crazy moments from 2010!

"Let's play some soccer!"

"I feel really sick, Nani!"

"I've just thrown up, mate!"

10 NEVILLE AND SCHOLES KISS!

Ever had an annoying aunt come round and give you a big sloppy kiss on the face? We reckon that's what it was like for Paul Scholes when Gary Neville got hold of him after their win over Man. City. Ewww!

9 HENRY GOES TO AMERICA!

Thierry Henry stunned the football world in July when he quit Spanish champions Barcelona to join the New York Red Bulls in the MLS!

8 EVRA & NANI THROW UP!

What the chunks had Patrice Evra and Nani been eating to make them chunder ON THE PITCH during Man. United's match against Tottenham last April? Probably a dodgy pie!

"I can't believe I didn't score!"

WORLD CUP FLOP!

"Which club am I at now?"

7 MESSI FORGETS HOW TO SCORE!

After netting more than 30 goals for Barca last season, many experts predicted Lionel Messi to hit double figures at the World Cup. But amazingly, he scored a big fat zero. Epic fail, Leo!

6 FULHAM ARE PREM'S BEST!

Well, kind of. Last season, the Cottagers got further in Europe than any English team as they reached the final of the Europa League. They even spanked Euro legends Juventus 4-1 on the way!

5 O'NEILL QUITS ASTON VILLA!

Days before the season started, most Villa fans were dreaming of Martin O'Neill leading them to a top four finish and the holy land of the Champions League. But no one told O'Neill – he resigned and left every Villa fan shaken. Ouch!

O SHOCKS!

ON TOP OF THE WORLD!

Nice prank, Pepe. Now take it off!

4 FORLAN IS THE WORLD CUP'S TOP PLAYER!

Before the World Cup, there was more chance of David Beckham appearing on The X Factor than there was of Diego Forlan being FIFA's Player of the Tournament. But amazingly, he won the prize thanks to his blinding matchplay!

3 FABREGAS IN A BARÇA SHIRT!

When Arsene Wenger saw this picture in his morning newspaper, he probably choked on his Coco Pops. Fabregas was keen on a transfer to Barcelona all summer and when the Spain lads stuck him in the shirt, Wenger would not have been happy!

That goal was miles in, ref!

2 WAZZA LIVING IN A CARAVAN!

When we first saw this photo, we thought it was just some weirdo who lives in a caravan, talks to pigeons and eats baked beans with his hands. But it was actually Wayne Rooney filming Nike's cool and thrilling World Cup TV advert!

1 LAMPARD'S GHOST GOAL!

The whole world saw Frank Lampard's goal-that-wasn't-given against the Germans – everyone apart from the ref and his two assistants, that is. Should've gone to Specsavers, lads!

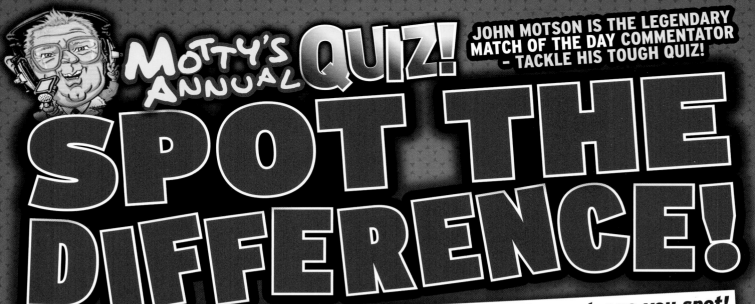

MOTTY'S ANNUAL QUIZ!

SPOT THE DIFFERENCE!

There are five changes in each pic – get two points for each one you spot!

(DON'T CHEAT!)

MY SCORE OUT OF 20

MORE QUIZ FUN ON PAGE 20!

WAYNE ROONEY
MAN. UNITED & ENGLAND

WORLD STAR!

PLAYER PROFILE

POSITION: Striker
AGE: 25
VALUE: £60 million
DID YOU KNOW?
Wazza scored his 100th Premier League goal in January 2009!

MATCH OF THE DAY

PREMIER LEAGUE 2010
TEAM OF THE YEAR!

MOTD picks the Premier League Team of the Year – find out who's made it in!

THE KEEPER!
PEPE REINA
LIVERPOOL

AGE: 28 **COUNTRY:** SPAIN

We love Pepe for two reasons – firstly, he's one of the biggest jokers in the Prem and is constantly merking his team-mates. Secondly, because he's a world-class keeper – his shot-stopping is breath-taking, his throwing and kicking are deadly accurate and he can save penalties with his eyes closed!

THE LEFT-BACK!
PATRICE EVRA
MAN. UNITED
AGE: 29
COUNTRY: FRANCE

All right, so he had a totally pants World Cup for France when he went on strike, but in the Prem Pat's an absolute beast – and that's why he's in our team of the year! He's a winger and a full-back all rolled into one, with his scuttling runs, demon crossing and wicked tackling!

THE RIGHT-BACK!
GLEN JOHNSON
LIVERPOOL
AGE: 26
COUNTRY: ENGLAND

Johnno used to be one of those attacking full-backs who was great going forward, but shocking at defending – but that's all changed now. He's better than most wingers when he's dribbling up the wing, and now he's ace at defending as well – with his tackling and positioning top-class!

LEE DIXON SAYS:
"Johnson's an athlete, he likes a tackle, he's not bad in the air, he's great going forward, he can cross a good ball and he scores goals now and then!"

THE CENTRE-BACK!
MICHAEL DAWSON
TOTTENHAM
AGE: 26 **COUNTRY:** ENGLAND

It feels like Daws has been around longer than that old bloke who lives down the road! But it's in the last 12 months that he's really blossomed – which resulted in a World Cup call-up. Awesome in the air, brave as a soldier and tackles for fun – that's what we love about him!

THE CENTRE-BACK!
THOMAS VERMAELEN
ARSENAL
AGE: 24 **COUNTRY:** BELGIUM

The Verminator took to the Prem like a duck to water in his first season. He's cool and calm on the ball and knows how to tackle – his left foot is so powerful, we've heard it was designed by a team of scientists in a top-secret bunker!

TURN OVER FOR MORE TEAM OF THE YEAR STARS!

THE LEFT-WINGER!
STEVEN GERRARD LIVERPOOL
AGE: 30 **COUNTRY:** ENGLAND

Yeah, we know he prefers to play in the middle – but in our team he's going to get a free role to cause absolute carnage. The Reds' skipper is the heartbeat of the Liverpool team and has been for ages. His surging runs, thumping shots and pinpoint passing would get your gran off her seat!

GARY LINEKER SAYS:
"Steven Gerrard is a great player – one of England's greatest – and has been for a long time. He leads by example!"

THE RIGHT-WINGER!
NANI MAN. UNITED
AGE: 23 **COUNTRY:** PORTUGAL

When most people see their best mate move away, they get sad and even, secretly, shed a few tears – but not the United trickster. He's come on leaps and bounds since Cristiano Ronaldo left Old Trafford. He's got the tricks, the speed, the confidence and now the end product to become one of the best in the world!

ALAN SHEARER SAYS:
"There is more to Lampard than just goals. For a start, only Cesc Fabregas got more assists in the Premier League last season and there's his hunger and desire too. He just keeps getting better!"

THE CENTRAL MIDFIELDER!
FRANK LAMPARD CHELSEA
AGE: 32 **COUNTRY:** ENGLAND

There's only one thing more certain than fish smelling of fish, and that's Lamps scoring 20 goals from midfield! He's been Chelsea's main man for the past five years and is showing no signs of fading away. His shooting is so powerful and accurate, it's actually quite scary!

THE CENTRAL MIDFIELDER!
CESC FABREGAS
ARSENAL
AGE: 23   COUNTRY: SPAIN

When we saw Cesc prancing about on stage after the World Cup with a Barcelona shirt on, we thought: "That's the last we've seen of him, then!" But thankfully it wasn't! He's the real deal this boy – mega skilful, a pass master, a goalscorer and an all-round legend!

GARTH CROOKS SAYS:
"The young Spaniard topped Arsenal's scoring charts last season and deserves to be at a club that is regularly winning things!"

THE STRIKER!
DIDIER DROGBA
CHELSEA
AGE: 32
COUNTRY: IVORY COAST

Last season's Golden Boot winner hit 29 goals in 32 Prem games. Yes, that's almost one goal every single game in the hardest league in the world – Drog's a machine! He's a deadly mix of muscle man, targetman and finisher – and that's why he's in our team of the year!

THE STRIKER!
WAYNE ROONEY
MAN. UNITED
AGE: 25
COUNTRY: ENGLAND

We know he bombed at the World Cup – but so did the whole England team. It's when he pulls on that famous red United shirt that he becomes unstoppable. What is a typical Wazza goal these days? A header, a volley, a chip, maybe a lob or a long-range blaster? Nope, it's all of them!

GARY LINEKER SAYS:
"Wayne Rooney is the sort of player you want at the centre of everything as he is one of the great players in football. He has great positional sense and is a terrific all-round player!"

TURN OVER TO PICK YOUR DREAM TEAM!

PICK YOUR 2010 DREAM TEAM!

ROONEY **DROGBA**

LAMPARD **FABREGAS**

GERRARD **NANI**

DAWSON **VERMAELEN**

EVRA **JOHNSON**

REINA

THIS IS MOTD'S PREMIER LEAGUE DREAM TEAM, NOW YOU CAN PICK YOUR TEAM!

CHOOSE WHOEVER YOU LIKE, BUT WE'VE GIVEN YOU SOME IDEAS!

KEEPERS!
Pepe Reina
Joe Hart
Heurelho Gomes
Brad Friedel
Shay Given
Paul Robinson
Edwin van der Sar

LEFT-BACKS!
Ashley Cole
Patrice Evra
Gareth Bale
Leighton Baines
Maynor Figueroa
Wayne Bridge
Gael Clichy

RIGHT-BACKS!
Glen Jonhson
Branislav Ivanovic
Bacary Sagna
Gary Neville
John Paintsil
Micah Richards
Vedran Corluka

CENTRE-BACKS!
Michael Dawson
Ledley King
Thomas Vermaelen
Nemanja Vidic
Brede Hangelaand
Richard Dunne
Ryan Nelsen

MIDFIELDERS!
Steven Gerrard
Frank Lampard
Cesc Fabregas
Wilson Palacios
Nigel de Jong
James Milner
Michael Essien
Paul Scholes

WINGERS!
Aaron Lennon
Antonio Valencia
Theo Walcott
Florent Malouda
Lee Chung-Yong
Steven Pienaar
Adam Johnson
Nani

STRIKERS!
Didier Drogba
Carlos Tevez
Bobby Zamora
Jermain Defoe
Wayne Rooney
Darren Bent
Fernando Torres

WRITE YOUR TEAM'S NAME HERE!

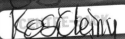

Fabianski

Clichy / Sagna

Koscielny / Vermaelen

Arshavin / Fabregas

Walcott / Nasri

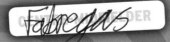

Van Persie

Chamakh

STEVEN GERRARD

LIVERPOOL & ENGLAND

WORLD STAR!

PLAYER PROFILE

POSITION: MIdfielder
AGE: 30
VALUE: £20 million
DID YOU KNOW?
Gerrard has played more than 500 games for Liverpool and England!

MOTTY'S ANNUAL QUIZ!

FROM TOP TO BOTTOM!

Match the top of the players to their bottom half!

Give yourself five points for each correct answer!

LOUIS SAHA

MIKEL ARTETA

JACK RODWELL

JERMAINE BECKFORD

PHIL NEVILLE

PUT YOUR ANSWER IN THESE BOXES!

THE LEGS OF...

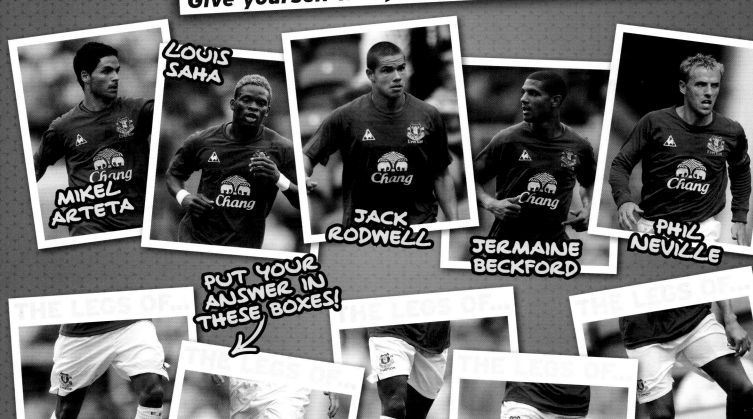

A

B

C

D

E

MORE QUIZ FUN ON PAGE 36!

(DON'T CHEAT!)

ANSWERS

Mikel Arteta – D, Louis Saha – C, Jack Rodwell – E, Jermaine Beckford – A, Phil Neville – B.

MY SCORE OUT OF 25

20

CRISTIANO RONALDO

REAL MADRID & PORTUGAL

PLAYER PROFILE

POSITION: Forward
AGE: 25
VALUE: £80 million
DID YOU KNOW?
Ronaldo bagged 26 league goals in his first season with Real!

MATCH OF THE DAY

WORLD STAR!

MY iPOD PLAYLIST!

The Prem's biggest stars tell us what they listen to in their spare time!

RIO FERDINAND MAN. UNITED

FERDINAND SAYS: "I love Wiley, he's a fantastic rapper, and I'm a friend of his as well. **Chipmunk** is also a great upcoming British hip-hop star. People don't understand how much young British talent we have – that's what I enjoy listening to more than anything!"

JOE COLE LIVERPOOL

COLE SAYS: "I've been a massive fan of Oasis for a long time and listen to them a lot on the coach and before games. I really like **The Killers** too – but if it's a big game then I'll go for a bit of Prodigy or something like that to get me pumped up!"

I'm a fan of the Kop Choir!

SHAUN WRIGHT-PHILIPS MAN. CITY

SWP SAYS: "Kayne West is fantastic and I like **Jay-Z** too. I listen to music I like before a match, but some lads listen to stuff that gets them fired up. Some players want to relax and some want music that gets them ready for a battle – it's just down to the player!"

DIDIER DROGBA
CHELSEA & IVORY COAST

WORLD STAR!

CUP 2010!
THE STORY IN PICTURES!

Gyan's gonna get ya, suckers!

GHANA RULED AFRICA UNTIL...
Ghana, led by goal-getter Asamoah Gyan, blitzed their opposition to reach the quarter-finals!

...SUAREZ DID THIS!
But Uruguay cheat Luiz Suarez punched the ball from the line to stop them making the semis!

SLAPHEAD SNEIJDER!
Wesley was as surprised as we were when he headed in for Holland as they dumped Brazil out of the tournament!

D'OH!

GERMANY 4 ARGENTINA 0!
Germany didn't just beat Argentina, they well and truly merked them. Their superkids were the stars of the tournament by a mile!

OUCH!
HOLLAND HIT OUT!
Things got well tasty in the final when Nigel de Jong started auditioning for a part in a Jackie Chan film!

VIVA ESPANA!
That wasn't enough to stop Spain marching to victory. They call their incredible passing style Tiki-Taka – and it's un-flipping-beatable!

TURN OVER FOR MORE WORLD CUP ACTION...

NEW WORLD STARS!

MOTD reveals the players you might not have known before the World Cup this year, but they're proper global superstars now!

MAGICAL MIDFIELD MASTER!

FABIO COENTRAO
PORTUGAL
**HE'S GONE FROM...
SPEEDY DEFENDER!
TO... DEADLY
ATTACKING FULL-BACK!**

Attacking full-backs are very much the future and this bloke is one of the finest there is. He dashes forward like a cheetah, carrying the ball left and right and slipping strikers in on goal!

MESUT OZIL
GERMANY
**HE'S GONE FROM...
LITTLE-KNOWN
FANCYMAN!
TO... WORLD-CLASS
PLAYMAKER!**

Ozil has all the talent to become a megastar. He dances around tackles, his final ball is always perfect and he can crack a ball in from far out as well – that's why Real Madrid bought him!

FLYING WING WIZARD!

THOMAS MULLER
GERMANY
HE'S GONE FROM... INVISIBLE STRIKER! TO... SILKY-SKILLED WIDE MAN!

Before the World Cup, Thomas was just a lad trying to play a few games for Bayern Munich – but after the World Cup, he was a full-on hero! Muller wowed the world – even England – with his daring runs and expert finishing!

LANDON DONOVAN
USA
HE'S GONE FROM... GREAT MIDFIELDER! TO... INFLUENTIAL GOALSCORER!

Donovan really stood out in South Africa. The ex-Everton midfielder had a bit of everything – great organisation, top passing and clinical finishing. He really saved the USA's butts!

DEADLY GOAL MACHINE!

TURBO CHARGED STAR!

ASAMOAH GYAN
GHANA
HE'S GONE FROM... PROMISING STRIKER! TO... DOMINATING TARGETMAN!

If there was a Busting A Gut For Your Country Award at the World Cup, Gyan would have won it. His fitness levels were top, his hold-up play immense and he scored some vital goals as Ghana charged to the quarters!

DIEGO FORLAN
URUGUAY
HE'S GONE FROM... LA LIGA HERO! TO... WORLD-CLASS ATTACKER!

Forlan's blond locks look like something out of a Hollywood action film, and his efforts in 2010 are worthy of a blockbuster. Somehow, he dragged his Uruguay team to the semis and he scored five goals!

TURN OVER FOR MORE WORLD CUP ACTION!

CRAZIEST WORLD CUP EVER!

MOTD checks out the tournament's wackiest moments and funniest things!

1 PAUL THE OCTOPUS: EXPERT PUNDIT!

Who'd have thought an octopus would predict results better than the MOTD boys? Paul was given two food boxes, each with a country's flag on it, and the box he ate from always won!

CRAZY RATING: ★ ★ ★ ★ ☆

DOMENECH BLANKED BY EVRA!

2 SCHWEINSTEIGER SHUFFLE!

We caught Germany megastar Bastian Schweinsteiger throwing some mega moves as he finished training. He was joining in with some local singers – and we were well impressed, Schweiny!

CRAZY RATING: ★ ★ ★ ☆ ☆

3 FRANCE SQUAD LOSE THE PLOT!

What a World Cup for Les Bleus. Nicolas Anelka told boss Raymond Domenech to stuff it, he was soon sent home, the team were not happy and captain Patrice Evra led a strike. You absolute plonker!

CRAZY RATING: ★ ★ ★ ★ ★

4 NEW ZEALAND ARE UNBEATABLE!

If you had predicted this before the tournament, you'd have LOL'd. But draws with Slovakia, Italy and Paraguay handed New Zealand the honour of being the only unbeaten team at the World Cup. Well done!

CRAZY RATING: ★ ★ ★ ★ ☆

ALL WHITES CONQUER THE WORLD!

5 BONKERS BALL!

The special Adidas Jabulani World Cup ball cost £80. Or you could pick up a £2 beach ball and have just the same effect – light, floaty and impossible to control. It was a nightmare for the keepers!

CRAZY RATING: ★★★☆☆

6 REALLY SILLY HAIR!

We think there were stylists who did players' hair in the dark. How else do you explain some of the World Cup's bad barnets – including this one from Cameroon's Rigobert Song? He's having a laugh!

CRAZY RATING: ★★★☆☆

7 CRAZY GOAL CELEBRATIONS!

It was impossible not to smile at South Africa's sick dancing, or laugh when Milan Jovanovic fell down a hole when he scored against Germany, or chuckle when Gabriel Heinze slapped a TV camera after it hit his face!

CRAZY RATING: ★★★★☆

8 X-RATED FINAL!

It started with a pitch invader getting a biffing from security, then moved on to Holland giving Spain a good old-fashioned roughing-up. But they failed and the slick Spaniards were champions of the world!

CRAZY RATING:

★★★☆☆

FANS OF THE WORLD!

THE DUDES IN THE STANDS WHO MADE US LAUGH...

COOKING POT!

GHANA

This dude cooks dinner on his head – he's the Jamie Oliver of Ghana, but with better teeth!

WRESTLING MASK!

MEXICO

Unfortunately, his special powers ran out in the second round when they came up against Argentina!

BRAZIL

Bag of oranges, Lionel Messi doll, two iced buns stuck to his head – this guy's ready to party!

MINI MESSI!

LOOKALIKES!

MOTD reveals the best likenesses in footy!

1

Fancy coming over to watch Villa, B.A.?

I ain't getting on no plane, J.C.!

JOHN CAREW
BRINGS HIS A-GAME!

B.A. BARACUS
JOINED THE A-TEAM!

2

JAMES MILNER
TO MAN. CITY FROM VILLA!

BUZZ LIGHTYEAR
TO INFINITY AND BEYOND!

3

Something smells fishy here!

It's your socks, Ozil!

MESUT OZIL
PASS, SHOOT, SCORE!

BLACK GOLDFISH
GLUG, GLUG, GLUG!

4

MICHAEL DAWSON
PLAYS WITH KING!

STUART BROAD
BOWLS WITH SWING!

5

BACARY SAGNA
RIGHT-BACK AT ARSENAL!

PAUL THE OCTOPUS
LEFT BACK IN THE FISH TANK!

6

Know any good tricks, mate?

Only in Quidditch, Wazza!

WAYNE ROONEY
WIZARD ON THE BALL!

SEAMUS FINNIGAN
WIZARD IN HARRY POTTER!

KAKA
REAL MADRID & BRAZIL

WORLD STAR!

GETTING READY!
The MOTD cameras are about to roll, so Jake practises his introduction to the show!

MAKING NOTES!
Shearer and Dixon go through their research notes before going live on air!

WINDOW CLEANERS CRASH THE SET!

What? Who's behind me?

That's not Paz and Bez is it?

We're on TV, dude!

Let's go for a re-take!

IN THE OUTSIDE BROADCAST TRUCK!
Lawro checks out the Outside Broadcast Truck – where all the TV angles and replays that you see on telly are selected!

WOAH! LOADS OF TELLIES!

MARK BRIGHT

JONATHAN PEARCE

MARK LAWRENSON

IN THE COMMENTARY BOX!
Mark Bright and Jonathan Pearce get to the commentary box well before kick-off. They swot up on the teams so they are experts on them!

JAKE HUMPHREY SAYS: "People don't realise that sports presenters write their own scripts for the show. I write it down and give it to the autocue operator, who types it into the autocue so I can read it when looking at the camera!"

WATCHING THE MOTD LADS!

LADS LISTEN IN!
The guys stay in the commentary box at half-time, and for a short while after full-time, so that they can listen to what Lineker and the boys say in the studio!

DAN WALKER SAYS: "Lawro eats bacon sandwiches before the show – he loves them!"

DAN WALKER

MOTTY'S ANNUAL QUIZ!
GUESS THE CLUB!

Use the clues below to name the four clubs!
Give yourself five points for each correct answer!

1

YOUR ANSWER

2

YOUR ANSWER

3

YOUR ANSWER

4

YOUR ANSWER

(DON'T CHEAT!)

MY SCORE OUT OF 20

ANSWERS
1 Sunderland, 2 West Ham,
3 Man. United, 4 Blackpool.

MORE QUIZ FUN ON PAGE 48!

36

MAROUANE CHAMAKH

ARSENAL & MOROCCO

WORLD STAR!

PLAYER PROFILE

POSITION: Striker
AGE: 26
VALUE: £15 million
DID YOU KNOW?
Chamakh was born in France, but plays footy for Morocco!

THE ULTIMATE
GOAL MA

LIONEL MESSI
BARCELONA
LAST SEASON 37 goals
GOAL AWARDS 2009-10 La Liga top scorer (34) & European Golden Shoe
2010-11 TARGET 40 goals
GOAL MISSION Jink past loads of defenders, race into the box and calmly finish!

CRISTIANO RONALDO
REAL MADRID
LAST SEASON 33 goals
GOAL AWARDS European Golden Shoe 2008 & Man. United record for most goals in a season (42)
2010-11 TARGET 40 goals
GOAL MISSION Hit amazing free-kicks and use pace and skills to make defenders cry!

GONZALO HIGUAIN
REAL MADRID
LAST SEASON 29 goals
GOAL AWARDS Real Madrid's top league scorer last season (27) and one of only three Argentina players to score a hat-trick in a World Cup
2010-11 TARGET 30 Goals
GOAL MISSION Spearhead the Real attack and use aerial ability and slick finishing to hurt teams!

DIDIER DROGBA
CHELSEA
LAST SEASON 37 goals
GOAL AWARDS 2009-10 Prem top scorer (29) & Ivory Coast all-time top scorer
2010-11 TARGET 30 goals
GOAL MISSION Use power to score from free-kicks, shake off defenders and blast shots past keepers!

ACHINES!

MOTD reveal the deadliest forwards with robot-like precision!

FERNANDO TORRES
LIVERPOOL
LAST SEASON 22 goals
GOAL AWARDS Liverpool's top scorer last season & fastest player in Livepool's history to score 50 league goals
2010-11 TARGET 30 goals
GOAL MISSION Play on the shoulder of the last defender and make lots of clever runs!

WAYNE ROONEY
MAN. UNITED
LAST SEASON 34 goals
GOAL AWARDS
Man. United's top scorer in each of past two seasons
2010-11 TARGET 35 goals
GOAL MISSION Create goals, get on the end of everything in the area and score all United's penalties!

DAVID VILLA
BARCELONA
LAST SEASON 28 goals
GOAL AWARDS Valencia top scorer for the past five years & Spain's all-time top scorer in World Cup matches (8)
2010-11 TARGET 35 goals
GOAL MISSION Finish everything that you get a sniff of. Drift out wide to get the ball when you need to!

MY FAVE THREE!
1st Walcott
2nd Nasri
3rd Chamakh

HE SAID

MOTD reveals the funniest, craziest

"Strikers are a bit like goalkeepers, aren't they?"

That's what footy pundit **Graeme Souness** said after Arsenal beat Porto. In the same way clowns are a bit like badgers, eh mate?

"He can start a fight in an empty barn!"

Birmingham boss **Alex McLeish** on Derby star, and BBC footy pundit, Robbie Savage!

"I've lived here for seven years and watched it twice – it's even worse than French TV!"

Arsenal's **Gael Clichy** hates EastEnders!

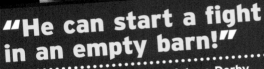

WATCH OUT GIRLS!

"I'll learn English by watching Coronation Street!"

But Man. City boss **Roberto Mancini** really loves Corrie!

"I prefer to kiss a beautiful lady rather than the badge!"

Chelsea boss **Carlo Ancelotti** doesn't like the way some Prem players kiss their footy shirts!

WHAT?

and weirdest quotes of the year!

> **"At full-time I'm like an irritated Jack Russell!"**
> Blackpool boss Ian Holloway wasn't happy with the draw at Crystal Palace!

BARKING MAD!

> **"It smells – I've only cleaned it once!"**
> Newcastle hero **Jonas Gutierrez** on his famous Spiderman mask (the mask he keeps in his pants by the way!)

> **"He got homesick for Glasgow – which is strange, considering that he's a Bulgarian!"**
> Martin O'Neill on why it took Stiliyan Petrov ages to settle at Aston Villa!

MARADONA'S MAD MOMENTS!
THE ARGENTINA LEGEND IS THE KING OF BONKERS QUOTES!

> **"I grew it because my dog almost ate my mouth and left me a big scar!"**
> ...on why he grew his new beard!

> **"We all know what the French are like and Platini, as a Frenchman thinks he knows it all!"**
> ...on France and its greatest football star!

> **"I'm not scared of anyone, unless they're wearing a mask!"**
> ...on the only thing he's frightened of!

> **"I have 23 wildcats prepared to leave their skins on the pitch!"**
> ...on his Argentina squad before the World Cup!

DIEGO'S GOT A BIG GOB!

BOGEY MONSTERS!

PICK IT, LICK IT, ROLL IT, FLICK IT!

These gross footy stars and managers just can't help digging for a greeny!

RUMMAGE!

KEVIN DAVIES
BOLTON
Wow! His finger is in up to his knuckle! He means business!

PEPE REINA
LIVERPOOL
Even his gloves don't stop Pepe going on a booger hunt!

JOGI LOW
GERMANY MANAGER
Are you sure he's not really called Bogey Low?

BOGEY ALERT!

MARTIN SKRTEL
LIVERPOOL
That's snot what we want to see from the Anfield hardman!

LITTLE GREEN MAN!

JERMAINE JENAS
TOTTENHAM
That's a real snot rocket from the midfield general!

BARRY FERGUSON
BIRMINGHAM
Quick! There's a booger on the loose!

BUT THE BOGEY KING IS...
SIR ALEX FERGUSON
The undoubted king of bogey hunting is Sir Alex Ferguson!

GOT IT!

CARLOS TEVEZ
MAN. CITY & ARGENTINA

WORLD STAR!

TOP 10 BEST...
GOALS O

10

FALCAO
PORTO
3 April 2010
Slamming in a mega overhead kick from 15 yards out is always impressive – especially when you torpedo it into the bottom corner with such force the helpless Maritimo keeper ends up in the back of the net crying like a little girl!

FANTASTIC FALCAO!

9

VAN'S TH MAN!

GIOVANNI VAN BRONCKHORST
HOLLAND 6 July 2010
When Gio began his waddle up field against Uruguay at the World Cup, we thought it was safe to send a few texts while he did his usual trick of shanking a cross into row Z. Little did we know he was about to hit one of the most amazing 40-yarders ever!

8

DINK!

MESSI MAULS THE GUNNERS!

LIONEL MESSI
BARCELONA
6 April 2010
There were so many great Messi goals in 2010 that it's difficult to pick one out! We've gone for this immense dink over Manuel Almunia's head as he tore Arsenal apart in the Champions League with an extra special, four-goal performance!

F 2010!

DAVID VILLA
SPAIN 21 June 2010

David Villa played a hide-and-seek game with the poor Honduras defenders, zig-zagging in and out of them with ease. He lost his balance as he took the shot, but that didn't stop his whipped finish nestling in the top corner. Good work!

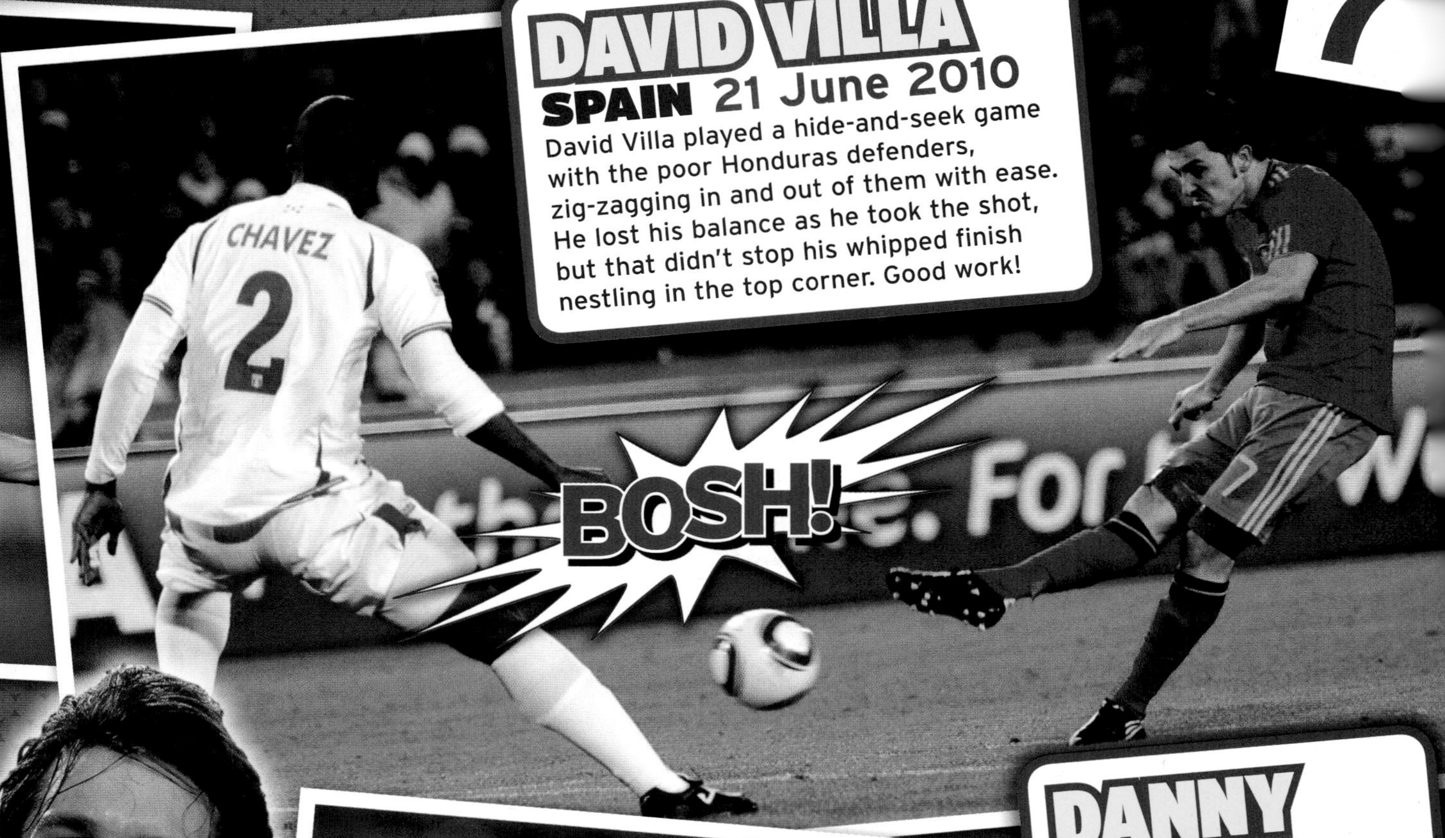

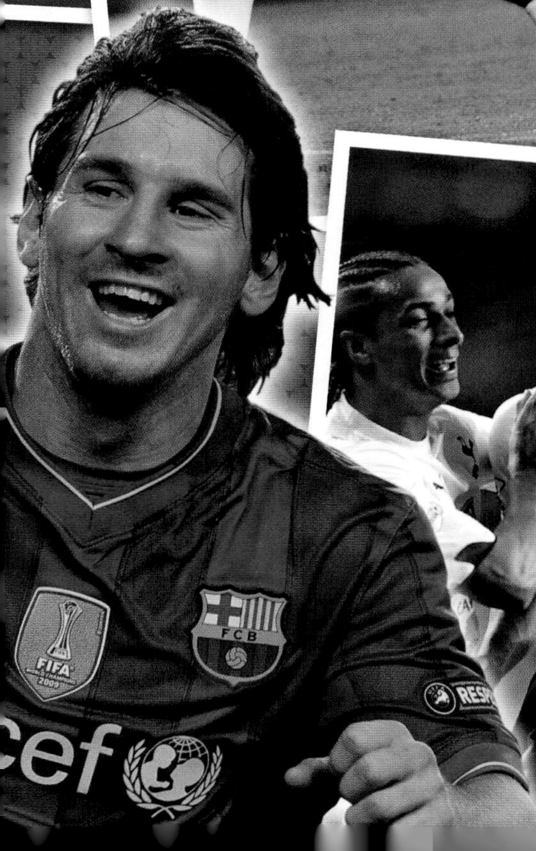

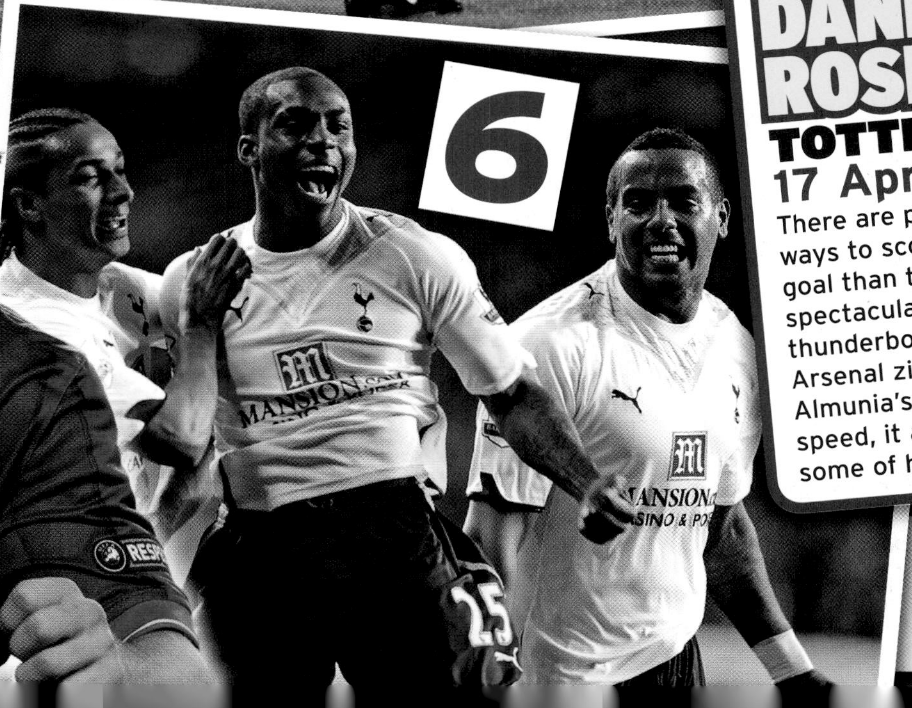

7

BOSH!

6

DANNY ROSE
TOTTENHAM
17 April 2010

There are probably easier ways to score your first ever goal than this, but none as spectacular. Danny Rose's thunderbolt volley against Arsenal zipped past Manuel Almunia's face at such speed, it actually nicked off some of his Spanish stubble!

TURN OVER FOR MORE INCREDIBLE GOALS!

8

ROCKET ROBBEN! ↓

5

DAVID SILVA
SPAIN 8 June 2010
Sometimes goals are just plain cruel – Spain's ping-pong passing ripped Poland to shreds like a lion ruining an antelope. David Silva got the tap in, but it was all about the cheeky swivel and lob from Andres Iniesta on the edge of the box!

4

ARJEN ROBBEN
BAYERN MUNICH
7 April 2010
Crosses that drop out of the sky from about 100ft are well hard to hit sweetly, unless you're Arjen Robben. He waited for it to drop, waited a bit more, then stroked a volley into the net to send Man. United out of Europe!

FERNANDO TORRES
LIVERPOOL 28 March 2010
When Torres picked up the ball on the left-wing, the Sunderland defenders must have been thinking "what's the worst that could happen?" How about he shimmies past you and curls a belter right into the top corner? Oh yes!

3

RED-HOT TORRES! ↑

THWACK!

2

LAMPARD LETS FLY!

DOINK!

FRANK LAMPARD
CHELSEA 25 April 2010
Just when you think you've seen everything Frank Lampard can do, he pulls this little beauty out the bag against Stoke. Stretching to reach an over-hit cross, Lamps scoops the ball back across goal and in with the outside of his foot — beautiful stuff!

1

RAAASSSSP!

MAICON
INTER MILAN 16 April 2010
We've all tried this, the difference is that our efforts usually end up smashing a window in the neighbour's greenhouse. Not Maicon! He gets our vote as the most bombastic goal of 2010 for an outrageous juggle on the edge of the Juventus box, before a smashtastic volley into the corner. Totally unstoppable!

DO YOU AGREE?
You can fill in your favourite goals of 2010 right here!

1st ...... Fabregas 29 Dec ......

2nd ...... Podolski 29 Dec ......

3rd ...... Klose 29 Dec ......

MOTTY'S ANNUAL QUIZ! MISSING STARS!

Name the five missing stars in these two team line-ups below. Two points for each correct answer!

EVERTON!

BACK ROW (left to right):
1 Victor Anichebe
2 Phil ....
3 Jack ....
4 Iain Turner
5 Diniyar Bilyaletdinov
6 James Vaughan

FRONT ROW (left to right):
7 Tony ....
8 Leon Osman
9 Mikel ....
10 Sylvain Distin
11 Leighton ....

ARSENAL!

BACK ROW (left to right):
1 Johan Djourou
2 Jack Wilshere
3 Thomas ....
4 Bacary ....
5 Jay Emmanuel-Thomas
6 Manuel Almunia

FRONT ROW (left to right):
7 Emmanuel Frimpong
8 Gael ....
9 Theo Walcott
10 Carlos ....
11 Thomas ....

(DON'T CHEAT!)

MY SCORE OUT OF 20

ANSWERS EVERTON 2 Phil Jagielka 3 Jack Rodwell 7 Tony Hibbert 9 Mikel Arteta 11 Leighton Baines ARSENAL 3 Thomas Vermaelen 4 Bacary Sagna 8 Gael Clichy 10 Carlos Vela 11 Thomas Rosicky

MORE QUIZ FUN ON PAGE 62!

RIO FERDINAND

MAN. UNITED & ENGLAND

WORLD STAR!

PLAYER PROFILE

POSITION: Defender
AGE: 31
VALUE: £20 million
DID YOU KNOW?
United paid Leeds
£30 million for Rio
in 2002 – a world
record for a defender!

MATCH OF THE DAY

FOOTY FUNNIES!

PART TWO!

FOOTBALLERS DO THE FUNNIEST THINGS...

Someone put pepper in my hankie!

Left a bit. No, right... no, left!

Please don't fart, Wazza!

MAN. UNITED TRY NEW TACTIC AT CORNERS...

Try kicking it in the goal!

HOWARD GIVES TIPS TO OPPOSITION STRIKERS...

CHELSEA ASSISTANT HAS WIG BLOWN OFF...

PARP!

Beans, boss!

That's better!

A TO Z OF 2010!

MOTD reveals the best moments of 2010!

A — AWARDS

2010 was the year that Wayne Rooney grabbed the PFA Player of the Year award after destroying teams with his explosive performances!

CHAM-PEO-NE! CHAM-PEO-NE! CHAM-PEO-NE!

Who's the daddy now?

B — BUST-UPS

There have a been many this year, but stop scrapping and start playing, lads!

D — DOUBLE

Chelsea won the Prem and FA Cup to do the double for the first time in their history!

C — COMEBACKS

2010 was full of them. Wigan came from 2-0 down to beat Arsenal 3-2. But the Gunners had their day later as they came from 3-0 behind to beat Bolton 4-2!

Take that, Gooners!

E — ENGLAND

It was a pants World Cup for England, but their youngsters — like Jack Wilshere — are now ready to take on the world!

Prepare to get Jack-ed!

F FANTASY FOOTY

Match of the Day's free online game, at www.MOTDmag.com, has gripped the nation!

MATCH OF THE DAY MAGAZINE ★★★★★★★★★★★★★
Fantasy Footy! ★★★★★★★★★★★★★

J JOSE MOURINHO

After winning loads of trophies with Inter, Jose is now the boss at Real Madrid!

The Special One rules!

bwin

G GERMANS

Germans love to shock the world. First Bayern Munich reached the Champions League final, then Germany came third at the World Cup!

Ready for a knees-up, Drog?

You bet, Ash!

H HAT-TRICKS

The hat-trick club is bulging after loads of goal action this year!

I can't stop scoring hat-tricks!

K KNEE SLIDES

This goal celebration is back in fashion and now everyone's doing it!

L LIONEL MESSI

Not only has Messi shown that he's the best player in the world, but possibly the best player ever!

You can't Mess with me!

unicef

I INTER MILAN

The greatest year in their history saw Inter win Serie A, the Coppa Italia and the Champions League!

TURN OVER FOR MORE A-Z ACTION!

M MATCH OF THE DAY

The UK's most popular football magazine – read by the stars – is still No.1!

MOTD mag rocks, dudes!

P PORTSMOUTH

Penniless, full of injuries and relegated, Portsmouth marched into the FA Cup final in one of the most amazing cup stories ever! What a team, eh?

We'll be back next season!

We never go down without a fight!

I'm Jav-ing a blast!

N NEW STARS

Javier Hernandez, Ramires and Marouane Chamakh were some of the new faces who burst onto the Prem!

Q QUOTA

Prem clubs can now only have 25 stars in their squad aged 21 or over, which means that some guys, like Owen Hargreaves, miss out!

But I wanna play!

R RECORD BREAKERS

Chelsea's 103 goals last season broke the Prem record for most goals scored in a campaign!

We kept the goals coming!

O OWN GOALS

No easy games in the Prem? There was when Portsmouth visited Old Trafford in February and three of Man. United's goals went in off Portsmouth players!

You're supposed to score for us, nitwits!

S SHOCKS

Reading beat Liverpool 2-1 at Anfield and Leeds sneaked a 1-0 win against Man. United at Old Trafford in the FA Cup!

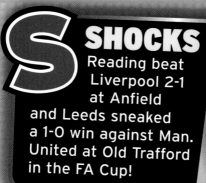

T TRANSFERS

You can't see through it, but everyone's favourite window is the transfer window. Man. City's millions always make it a tasty time of year!

City bought me for £24m!

SILVA
21

W WONDER GOALS

You know when you've seen a wonder goal when you shout BOOM when it hits the back of the net!

Here comes the Torr-nado!

X XTRA

MOTD XTRA launched in 2010 on **MOTDmag.com**, bringing you podcasts, videos and loads of behind-the-scenes exclusives!

MOTD XTRA!

U UNDER-17S

England Under-17s became European Champions after beating Spain 2-1 in the final!

EN-GER-LAND! EN-GER-LAND!

WINNERS
FA U17 CHAMPIONSHIP - LIECHTENSTEIN 2

Y YELLOW CARDS

English ref Howard Webb whipped out a world record 14 yellow cards in the World Cup final!

V VUVUZELAS

Love them or hate them, they were the sound of the 2010 World Cup!

Z ZIGIC

Peter Crouch finally has someone to look up to now that Birmingham have Nikola Zigic – the tallest player in the Prem!

2010'S BIGGEST...
CRY BABIES!

There has been loads of blubbin' on the pitch in 2010 – **MOTD** reveals the biggest cry babies of the year!

JAVIER ZANETTI INTER MILAN

The Inter captain is in floods of tears, but he's just won the Champions League!

ASAMOAH GYAN GHANA

Give it a rest, mate!

Fluffing a crucial World Cup penalty was too much for this bawling buffoon!

RYAN SHAWCROSS STOKE

I want my mummy!

Ryan's big and tough, but sometimes he just wants a cuddle from mummy!

ARTURO VIDAL CHILE

This dude waterlogged the grass after Chile went out of the World Cup!

ZOLTAN GERA FULHAM

Cheer up, mate – Fulham will reach the Europa League final again. Maybe!

3 WAYS TO MAKE A PLAYER CRY!

1 SWAP HIS FERRARI FOR

MAKE HIM CLEAN

DAVID VILLA

BARCELONA & SPAIN

WORLD STAR!

SECRETS OF THE STARS!

MOTD uncovers the stories the stars don't want you to know!

Need some singing tips, Beyonce?

FOSTER SINGS BEYONCE SONGS!

It's a well-known fact that footy stars have to sing a song to their team-mates when they sign for a new club, but most of them don't plump for a Beyonce classic! That's what Ben Foster did when he joined Birmingham – he told us he hit every high note and it sounded beautiful. Yeah right, Ben!

YOU'RE FIRED!

ASHLEY LOVES THE APRENTICE!

If you think most footballers spend their afternoons chilling out on the sofa watching re-runs of MTV Cribs, you're wrong. Ashley Young told us he loves nothing better than whacking on The Apprentice and watching Alan Sugar get nasty!

GETTING RATTY!

Tree-climbing, building dens, we've all had a stab at crazy stuff. But rat-catching, surely that's too far? Not if you're Shay Given – in an interview with **MOTD** mag the keeper revealed he used to run around his farm in Ireland, grabbing the pests!

GIVEN IS A RAT-CATCHER!

Snakes alive!

LAMPARD IS SCARED OF SNAKES!

You'd think avoiding snakes would be pretty easy – just stay clear of forests, swamps and jungles and you'll be okay. But Frank's agent owns a cobra, so whenever he goes round to talk to him, he has to confront his biggest fear!

David James says he spends all his away trips hammering Mario Kart on the Nintendo DS. So he must be pretty handy by now, right? Wrong! Jamo admitted to us just the other day that he's total guff. "I'm rubbish – I've got no stars and if you don't have stars your kart is really slow," he told us!

I'd better stick to footy!

JAMO IS RUBBISH AT MARIO KART!

SWP is known for his love of computer games, but did you know he dabbles in DJ-ing as well? The little man says he serves up a mix of RnB, funky house and old-school garage. He could be coming to a school disco near you very soon!

MAGIC MIXER!

SWP IS A SECRET DJ!

I saw him do it!

BOLTON BASH UP SPORTS CAR!

Here's a tip for any Premier League footballer visiting Bolton's training ground: don't park next to Gretar Steinsson! As revealed exclusively to **Match of the Day** magazine by Gary Cahill, Steinsson once rammed his motor into Nicky Hunt's brand new Lamborghini. Triple cringe, Gretar!

FOOTY FASHION!
WHO'S THE COOLEST?

These footy stars are rockin' the same style – but tell us who wears it best!

I look like a penguin!

THE COOLEST!

In your dreams, Nic!

My cap's way cooler than yours, Diouf!

THE COOLEST!

THE HIP-HOP LOOK!

NICOLAS ANELKA CHELSEA **V** **EL-HADJI DIOUF** BLACKBURN

THE BUSINESS SUIT!

SHAUN WRIGHT-PHILLIPS MAN. CITY **V** **STEVEN GERRARD** LIVERPOOL

I got dressed in the dark!

THE COOLEST!

MOTD verdict: It may look like Dioufy's dog has ripped his jeans to shreds, but the Blackburn man's got his swagger on. Anelka, on the other hand, looks like he's posing for his school photo!

MOTD verdict: OMG! Shauny, Shauny, Shauny – what is going on? You've either borrowed James Corden's suit or you need to get properly measured for it next time! But Stevie G looks well sharp!

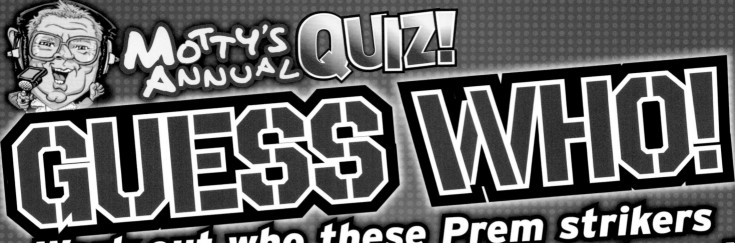

MOTTY'S ANNUAL QUIZ!
GUESS WHO!

Work out who these Prem strikers are and get two points for each one!

1
2
3
4
5

(DON'T CHEAT!)
MY SCORE
OUT OF 10

ANSWERS 1. Darren Bent (Sunderland) 2. Kevin Doyle (Wolves) 3. Peter Crouch (Tottenham) 4. Louis Saha (Everton) 5. Gabriel Agbonlahor (Aston Villa)

MORE QUIZ FUN
ON PAGE 74!

WESLEY SNEIJDER

INTER MILAN & HOLLAND

WORLD STAR!

PLAYER PROFILE
POSITION: Midfielder
AGE: 26
VALUE: £25 million
DID YOU KNOW?
Sneijder was Man of the Match four times at the 2010 World Cup!

MATCH OF THE DAY

8 BONKERS QUESTIONS FOR....

The Tottenham and England star tells MOTD about Facebook, mice and making his bed!

1 HAVE YOU EVER HAD A FIGHT WITH AN ANIMAL?

CROUCH SAYS: "The closest I've come to doing that is chasing a mouse round my kitchen for a good half an hour – I think the mouse came out on top because it managed to escape!"

2 HOW MANY PAIRS OF TRAINERS HAVE YOU GOT?

CROUCH SAYS: "I'm lucky because Puma give me trainers for free – so I'd say I'm pretty well stocked"

3 CAN YOU SAY ANYTHING IN FRENCH?

CROUCH SAYS: "We had a few French lads at Porstmouth and I'd take the mick by saying random French words – they always got angry! I'd to say 'Bon, la plage deux', which doesn't make sense – it means 'good, the beach two'. It used to wind them up!"

4 WHAT ARE YOU MOST SCARED OF?

CROUCH SAYS: "Apart from mice? I've got a new cinema room in my house and I put a scary film on in there the other day, but had to turn it off and put it on the normal telly because it was too much! The surround sound system was really scary!"

5 WHEN WAS THE LAST TIME YOU GOT IN TROUBLE?

CROUCH SAYS: "That was for my untidiness around the house – I'm always getting told off for things like leaving towels lying around and not making the bed!"

GET YOUR ROOM CLEANED!

ERS IONS PETER CROUCH!

6 WHICH PREM STAR WOULD YOU REJECT A FACEBOOK REQUEST FROM?

CROUCH SAYS: "It'd have to be David Bentley because he'd never stop chatting to me. I'd constantly be getting messages from him and I get enough of him talking at me in training!"

SHUT IT DAVID!

7 WHAT'S THE BEST FOOTBALL CHANT YOU'VE EVER HEARD?

CROUCH SAYS: "There was one at Liverpool that went 'Don't blame it on the Hamann, don't blame it on the Finnan, don't blame it on the Biscan, blame it on Traore' to the tune of Blame It On The Boogie by Michael Jackson. That was easily the funniest!"

8 WHO IS THE BIGGEST JOKER IN FOOTBALL?

CROUCH SAYS: "I think David James – he was part of that gang who used to pretend to speak French at Portsmouth and he was always making us laugh!"

DID YOU KNOW?
Crouch has played for ten different clubs during his professional career!

PREMIER LEAGUE SUPERKIDS!

SKILLS KING!

JACK WILSHERE

AGE: 18
CLUB: Arsenal
COUNTRY: England
POSITION: Midfielder
TOP SKILL: Clever passing

The Gunner's youngest ever league player is being trained to be the next Cesc Fabregas!

ENGLAND HERO!

GAEL KAKUTA

AGE: 19 **CLUB:** Chelsea
POSITION: Left winger/forward
COUNTRY: France
TOP SKILL: Skinning players

Kakuta's got all the skills of an experienced pro and his left foot is more dangerous than an angry tiger!

JACK RODWELL

AGE: 19 **CLUB:** Everton
POSITION: Midfielder
COUNTRY: England
TOP SKILL: Box-to-box running

Rodwell plays just like Steven Gerrard and could be just as amazing as the England hero!

DANIEL PACHECO

AGE: 19
POSITION: Striker
CLUB: Liverpool
COUNTRY: Spain
TOP SKILL: Outrageous trickery

This lad has more tricks than a magician and an eye for goal that helped Spain win the U19 Euros!

GOAL MACHINE!

PHIL JONES

AGE: 18
CLUB: Blackburn
POSITION: Centre-back
COUNTRY: England
TOP SKILL: Fierce tackling

If a car hit Phil, it'd bounce off. He's been linked with Man. United and could be an England regular soon!

WRITE YOUR ANSWER HERE!

I THINK THE BEST PLAYER IS:

....

DAVID BECKHAM

LA GALAXY & ENGLAND

PLAYER PROFILE

POSITION: Midfielder
AGE: 35
VALUE: £5 million
DID YOU KNOW?
Becks won the Premier League six times with Man. United!

MATCH OF THE **DAY**

WORLD STAR!

SOCCER ST[I

Argh, I've got stage fright!

WHAT IS A STEREOTYPE?

DICTIONARY SAYS: Something a group of people believe about another group – it's usually wrong or too simple!

ENGLAND

Long-ball merchants who always struggle to do anything on the big stage!

SPAIN

Pass, pass, pass, pass, pass, pass, pass, shoot, goal!

I'm the next Tom Daley!

BRAZIL

Showboaters, tricksters and free-kick kings!

PORTUGAL

Long hair, loads and loads of gel – they love to dive!

What me? Cheat? No way, amigos!

ARGENTINA

Watch out for their sneaky fouls, shirt pulls – and amazing forwards!

GHANA

Fast, great team spirit – but well dodgy keeper!

EREOTYPES!

NORWAY

Team full of giants who love the snow and ice!

RUSSIA

Andrey Arshavin and ten other unknowns with long names!

GERMANY

Love sausages, always get to the semis – and annoyingly good at penalty shootouts!

SOUTH KOREA

Little dudes, well organised, full of unbelievable energy and running!

INDIA

Football, what's football? It's all about cricket!

ITALY

Male models who love defending – boring to watch!

AUSTRALIA

Full of kangaroos, Prem rejects and over-the-hill players!

TOP 5
TRANSFERS OF 2010!

5

JAVIER HERNANDEZ
£6 million

THE DEAL: CHIVAS TO MAN. UNITED

When this deal went through, United fans screamed "Javier who?" But after watching the Mexico striker score two cracking goals at the World Cup, they were all singing his name!

MOTD RATING: ★★★☆☆

4

FREE!

JOE COLE

THE DEAL: CHELSEA TO LIVERPOOL

Reds boss Roy Hodgson is so crafty and wise, he nabbed the England star on a free transfer! We don't know how he did it, but we reckon Harry Potter's magic wand must have been involved!

MOTD RATING: ★★★☆☆

3

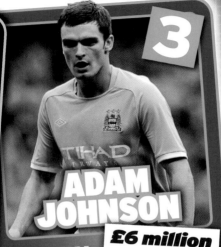

ADAM JOHNSON
£6 million

THE DEAL: BORO TO MAN. CITY

Is it too much to say this guy is the future of English football? Too late, we just said it! Johnson outshone City's foreign stars when he signed in January – the winger looks the real deal!

MOTD RATING: ★★★★☆

2

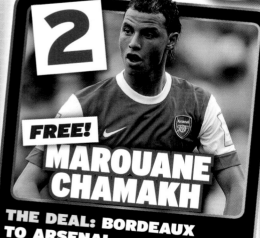

FREE!

MAROUANE CHAMAKH

THE DEAL: BORDEAUX TO ARSENAL

Just when you think Arsene Wenger has lost the plot he pulls this one out of the bag. Chamakh spent last season terrorising Champions League defenders for Bordeaux before rocking up at Arsenal for free. Nice work!

MOTD RATING: ★★★★☆

1 **DAVID VILLA**

THE DEAL: VALENCIA TO BARCELONA

You don't have to be a genius to work out this is a good deal. Sure, he cost a fair whack, but David Villa is the deadliest and most dependable striker on the planet. On the day of his signing there were reports of mass pant-wenting by La Liga defenders!

MOTD RATING:
★★★★★

£34 million for me? Bargain!

£34 million

CESC FABREGAS
ARSENAL & SPAIN

WORLD STAR!

Fly Emirates

World's top... TRICKSTERS!

MOTD picks the most skilful players in the world and explains what makes them so good!

LIONEL MESSI Why he's sick...

MAGIC MESSI DRIBBLE!

GET HIS GAME...

● Your control must be razor-sharp to dribble like Messi. Find a wall and pelt the ball at it – when it flies back, use one touch to control it!
● A change in direction will throw your marker, so practise running with the ball weaving quickly in and out of obstacles!
● Don't stay on the ball for too long – work space for a shot or a pass and get it done fast!

SKILL 1: UNBELIEVABLE DRIBBLING!

It's all about the rapid change in direction – he's like a slalom skier when he gets going and defenders can't guess what he'll do next!

SKILL 2: TOUCH OF A GENIUS!

If Messi tells the ball to do something, it just gets on and does it – he's got total, magical control over its every move!

SKILL 3: THE BIG WHIPPERS!

His trademark finish these days is one of those stinging curlers into the corner – he gives it one sharp flick with the inside of his boot to create the curl to beat the keeper!

MESUT OZIL Why he's sick...

CRAFTY REVERSE PASS!

GET HIS GAME...
- Use your first touch to cushion the ball into space – this will make it easier for you to control your pass!
- Practise hitting the ball with the outside of your foot – it's a good way of disguising passes!
- Give your marker 'the eyes' – look one way and send the pass off in another direction!

CRISTIANO RONALDO Why he's sick...

THE CHOP AND RUN!

GET HIS GAME...
- Perfect your ability to run at speed with the ball – prod it sharply forward in short bursts as you sprint!
- Stand on the spot and flick the ball behind your standing leg with the inside of your other foot!
- Once you've mastered this, do it on the run. Change direction quickly as you chop and sprint off with the ball!

ROBINHO Why he's sick...

GET HIS GAME...
- Body movement is the key here – get in front of a mirror and practise faking to go one way then the next just using your upper body!
- Now stick a ball down and arc your leg over the ball in the same way as your body!
- Now go outside into some open space and combine your moves as you dribble the ball at one of your mates!

RAPID STEPOVERS!

DAVID VILLA Why he's sick...

THE CHEEKY DINK!

GET HIS GAME...
- Get your technique right first – stab your foot under the ball to give it some height!
- Now aim for a target – get an old bin down the park and chip the ball in from distance!
- Time for a keeper now – get a mate to run out at you as you advance on goal, then dink it over him into the net!

TOP 5 INTERNET SKILLSTERS!

Search for these guys pulling off mind-bending tricks online!

1 Juan Mata
CLUB: Valencia
COUNTRY: Spain
BEST SKILL: Rabona nutmeg!

2 Keisuke Honda
CLUB: CSKA Moscow
COUNTRY: Japan
BEST SKILL: Cruyff turn!

3 Juan Riquelme
CLUB: Boca Juniors
COUNTRY: Argentina
BEST SKILL: Double dragback!

4 Ricardo Quaresma
CLUB: Besiktas
COUNTRY: Portugal
BEST SKILL: Curling screamers!

5 Zlatan Ibrahimovic
CLUB: Barcelona
COUNTRY: Sweden
BEST SKILL: Backheel volley!

MOTTY'S ANNUAL QUIZ! 2010 TEST!

Can you remember the craziest bits from 2010? Give yourself five points for every one you get right!

1 What did Spurs players pour over Harry Redknapp when they qualified for the Champions League?

A A BOWL OF CUSTARD! ☐
B STINKY OLD RUBBISH! ☐
C BARREL OF WATER! ☐

2 Which Prem superstar did Jedward hang out with in 2010?

A WAYNE ROONEY ☐
B PHIL JAGIELKA ☐
C TITUS BRAMBLE ☐

3 What is Sir Alex Ferguson talking about here?

I thought a horse show had been held on it!

4 Theo Walcott missd out on the World Cup squad in 2010, but what's his favourite TV programme?

A HOW TO LOOK GOOD NAKED! ☐
B DOCTOR WHO! ☐
C TOP GEAR! ☐

5 What kept David Beckham out of the World Cup?

A TOOTHACHE! ☐
B ANKLE-KNACK! ☐
C EARACHE! ☐

6 Everton signed Landon Donovan on loan in 2010 – which country does he play for?

A BRAZIL ☐
B TURKEY ☐
C USA ☐

7 How many goals did Leo Messi score against Arsenal at the Nou Camp?

A3 ☐ B4 ☐ C5 ☐

8 Which computer game was big with Prem stars in 2010?

A CALL OF DUTY ☐
B PEGGLE ☐
C POKEMON ☐

9 Who is this?

10 How many penalties were missed in the 2010 FA Cup Final?

A1 ☐ B2 ☐ C3 ☐

(DON'T CHEAT!) **MY SCORE OUT OF 50** ☐

ANSWERS
1C, 2A, 3 Wembley pitch, 4C, 5B, 6C, 7B, 8A, 9 Jose Mourinho 10 B.

MORE QUIZ FUN ON PAGE 80!

JOE HART

MAN. CITY & ENGLAND

WORLD STAR!

PLAYER PROFILE

POSITION: Keeper
AGE: 23
VALUE: £10 million
DID YOU KNOW?
Joe was named
Birmingham's Player of
the Year last season!

MATCH OF THE DAY

WHEN MANAGERS WERE PLAYERS!

Check out these funny old pics of managers when they were players! Write down who you think they are!

1 This super Scot has won loads of trophies!

I think it's............................

Och, man – skipping's fer girls!

Maybe I should-a look at the ball!

3 Don't take the Mick out of this boss!

I think it's............................

This moustache really tickles!

PHILIPS

2 He's wearing white, but he's a big Blue now!

I think it's............................

4 He likes to spend time at the seaside!

I think it's..........................

5 This boss really Spurs on his players!

I think it's..........................

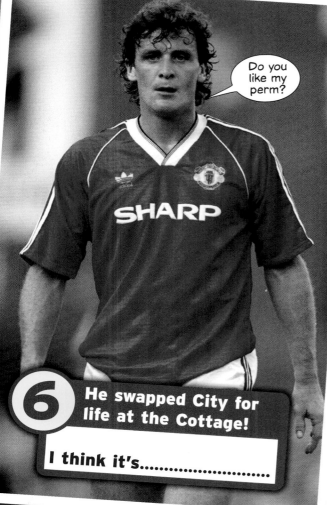

6 He swapped City for life at the Cottage!

I think it's..........................

7 This manager likes to eat Toffees!

I think it's..........................

ANSWERS! 1 Sir Alex Ferguson (Man. United), 2 Carlo Ancelotti (Chelsea), 3 Mick McCarthy (Wolves), 4 Ian Holloway (Blackpool), 5 Harry Redknapp (Tottenham) 6 Mark Hughes (Fulham); 7 David Moyes (Everton).

CAUGHT ON CAMERA!

We reveal the funniest stuff the MOTD cameras have spotted this year!

Smile, lads!

Get out of the way, ref!

REF TACKLED AT BOLTON!

Arms crossed, everyone!

ARSENAL MASCOT COPIES WENGER!

OUCH!

You'd better hope I don't fart!

BURNLEY KEEPER HEADBUTTS BUM!

FULLER INVADES...

BUMP!

...THE CROWD!

ZZZZzzzzz

WEST HAM STEWARD TAKES A NAP!

Got a letter E, anyone?

POMPEY STAR OWUSU-ABEYIE NEEDS A LETTER!

BRUSH! BRUSH!

CHELSEA FAN BRUSHES TEETH IN THE CROWD!

WORLD STAR!

BASTIAN SCHWEINSTEIGER

BAYERN MUNICH & GERMANY

PLAYER PROFILE

POSITION: Midfielder
AGE: 26
VALUE: £20 million
DID YOU KNOW?
He's played over 80 games for Germany — and he's only 26!

MATCH OF THE DAY

MOTTY'S ANNUAL QUIZ!
GUESS THE KIT?

Can you work out which Prem clubs used to wear these shirts?

1 ....

2 ....

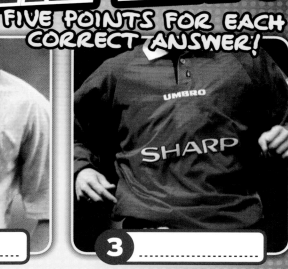

3 ....

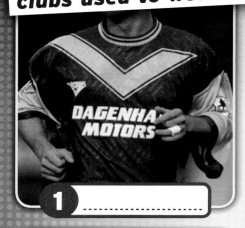

4 ....

5 ....

6 ....

7 ....

8 ....

9 ....

LUKA MODRIC

TOTTENHAM & CROATIA

WORLD STAR!

PLAYER PROFILE

POSITION: Midfielder
AGE: 25
VALUE: £20 million
DID YOU KNOW?
Luka won the Croatian league three years in a row with Dinamo Zagreb!

MATCH OF THE DAY

GARY LINEKER...
FOOTY HERO!

Take a look back at Match of the Day star Gary Lineker's awesome footy career!

LEICESTER LAD!

1 Gary joined his local club Leicester right after leaving school. He became a well deadly striker and scored loads of goals for the Foxes!

....

LECIESTER 1978-1985
GAMES: 194
GOALS: 95

TOP TOFFEE!

2 Lineker moved to Everton for £800,000 in 1985 and bagged an amazing 38 goals in his first season at Goodison Park!

....

EVERTON 1985-86
GAMES: 52   **GOALS:** 38

ENGLAND HERO!

3 Gary first played for England in 1984 and scored a total of ten goals at the 1986 and 1990 World Cup finals. He's England's second-highest goalscorer ever!

....

ENGLAND 1984-1992,
GAMES: 80   **GOALS:** 48

DID YOU KNOW?
Gary was the top scorer at the 1986 World Cup finals with six goals!

BARCA BOY!

4 After the 1986 World Cup, Gary left Everton and joined Barcelona in Spain for a mega £2.2 million! He scored an amazing 21 goals in his first season!

BARCELONA 1986-89
GAMES: 138 **GOALS:** 52

DID YOU KNOW?
Gary was voted Leicester's greatest ever player by the fans in 2009!

SPURS STAR!

5 Gary came back to England in 1989 and smashed in the goals during three seasons at White Hart Lane. He also won the FA Cup with Spurs in 1991!

TOTTENHAM 1989-1992
GAMES: 148
GOALS: 80

DID YOU KNOW?
Gary won the Golden Boot with three different English clubs – a national record!

GRAMPUS GREAT!

6 Surprisingly, Lineker finished his incredible career playing for Grampus Eight in Japan. He struggled with injury, but the J.League fans still loved seeing a footy legend!

GRAMPUS EIGHT 1992-94
GAMES: 18 **GOALS:** 4

WHO ARE YOU?

There's only one way to find out which type of player you are – take **MOTD**'s wicked test!

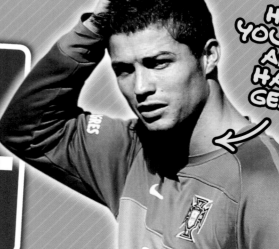

Q1
Your alarm clock goes off, it's time to get up! What do you do?

A: Put some music on and dance your way to the shower! ☐
B: Just do what Cristiano Ronaldo would do – find the hair gel! ☐
C: Find something to tackle and tackle it! 'Ave it! ☐
D: Oh no! You've slept in, you're late. What a doofus! ☐

Q2
It's pre-match meal time – what's on your plate?

A: A plateful of smooth tunes for you! It's time for a dance! ☐
B: You need to phone Cristiano Ronaldo to see what he's having! ☐
C: You don't care! You'll eat anything – even if it's alive! 'Ave it! ☐
D: You were too slow getting to the canteen – it's shut! What a doofus! ☐

Q3
It's ten minutes to kick-off, what are you doing?

A: The music is pumping and you're throwing some serious shapes! ☐
B: You're putting the finishing touches to your hair – just like Cristiano would be! ☐
C: Geeing the lads up and punching walls! 'Ave it! ☐
D: You took the wrong bus and ended up in the local supermarket! What a doofus! ☐

HAVE YOU GOT ANY HAIR GEL?

I'M GETTING HUNGRY!

GET YOUR HEAD ON IT!

Q5 The ball gets crossed into the box – what do you do?

A: Wait on the edge of the area so you can pounce on a fluffed clearance! ☐
B: Pull off a Cristiano Ronaldo-style volley into the top corner! ☐
C: Keep your eyes on the ball and launch your head at it! 'Ave it! ☐
D: You're too busy tying your shoelaces to notice! What a doofus! ☐

Q4 You score a last-minute winner – how do you celebrate?

A: You're a dancer, baby! It's time to get your groove on! ☐
B: Just do what Cristiano Ronaldo would do – milk the applause! ☐
C: Kiss the badge and give it the big roar! 'Ave it! ☐
D: Ha-ha... as if you'd score a goal! It was all a dream. What a doofus! ☐

Q6 Finally, if you were an animal what would you be?

A: Crocodile! You're constantly snapping away! ☐
B: A peacock! You love strutting around like Ronaldo! ☐
C: A lion – because you're a lionheart, roar! 'Ave it! ☐
D: A cross-eyed giant tortoise! Slow, clumsy and in no way dangerous! ☐

WHAT DID YOU PICK?

MOSTLY A
YOU ARE... YAYA TOURE!
Classic defensive midfielder – but you're just as famous for your dancing as you are for snapping into crunching tackles!

MOSTLY B
YOU ARE... NANI!
Or as you like to be known, the New Ronaldo! You've undoubtedly got the tricks – but you've also got the confidence to match!

MOSTLY C
YOU ARE... JOHN TERRY!
You're rock hard, you're totally passionate and you're a leader who wants to win! 'Ave it!

MOSTLY D
YOU ARE... EMILE HESKEY!
You're probably a nice person – it's a shame that you're a bit of a doofus!

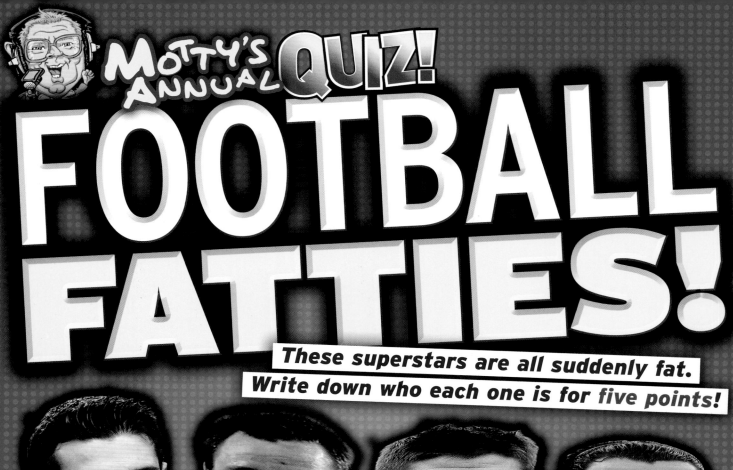

MOTTY'S ANNUAL QUIZ!
FOOTBALL FATTIES!

These superstars are all suddenly fat. Write down who each one is for five points!

1 WHO AM I?

2 WHO AM I?

3 WHO AM I?

4 WHO AM I?

5 WHO AM I?

6 WHO AM I?

7 WHO AM I?

8 WHO AM I?

9 WHO AM I?

10 WHO AM I?

11 WHO AM I?

12 WHO AM I?

FIND OUT YOUR TOTAL SCORE ON PAGE 92!

(DON'T CHEAT!)

ANSWERS 1 Robin van Persie, 2 John Terry, 3 Steven Gerrard, 4 Carlos Tevez, 5 Tim Cahill, 6 Ashley Young, 7 Kevin Nolan, 8 Aaron Lennon, 9 Wayne Rooney, 10 Darren Fletcher, 11 Barry Ferguson, 12 Danny Murphy.

MY SCORE OUT OF 60

LUIS FABIANO
SEVILLA & BRAZIL

PLAYER PROFILE

POSITION: Striker
AGE: 29
VALUE: £18 million
DID YOU KNOW?
Fabiano scored three goals for Brazil at the 2010 World Cup!

MATCH OF THE **DAY**

Joma

12bet.com

WORLD STAR!

PAZ AND BEZ'S... MOTD XTRA! BEST OF 2010!

The MOTD Xtra presenters look back on an incredible year!

READ IT FIRST! HEAR IT FIRST! SEE IT FIRST!

GETTING READY FOR THE SHOW!

BEZ SAYS: "You might think presenting an Internet footy show is just about turning up, larking around for 20 minutes then shooting off down the park for a kickabout – but you're wrong! We spend hours every week coming up with funny ideas, interviewing footy stars and writing scripts. It's awesome fun!"

Is it too late to replace Paz with Harry Hill?

BEZ ON TV!

PAZ SAYS: "BBC News love MOTD Xtra so much they asked Bez to talk about the World Cup. He did well – he didn't guff or anything and he said New Zealand would be a tough game for Italy. We ripped him at the time, but he was right – I think he got lucky with that!"

WORLD CUP 2010 DRAW

MOTD rocks. Right lads?

CHOOSING A WORLD CUP SONG!

PAZ SAYS: "When Rik Mayall found out his song Noble England had been voted the official MOTD Xtra World Cup song, he stormed into the studio, called me a twerp and chucked me out! The man is 100% barmy – at one point he chucked a load of pound coins on the floor and told us to pick them up and go and have fun!"

BEZ SAYS: "I loved it when Rik came in for that photoshoot! He was a total prankster – he was cracking us up with his bonkers poses!"

Where's my kit then, dudes?

WHO ARE PAZ & BEZ?

Top footy reporters – they spend their time camped out at the biggest Prem clubs getting the hottest stories... AND they present **MOTD Xtra**, the mega podcast and video series from MOTD magazine!

PAZ has got the most incredible hairstyle in football – it takes three hours and four tubs of wax to style, it's won 17 awards and can also be used to clean the toilet!

SUPPORTS... Shrewsbury
TOP SKILL... Writing gags!
RATES... Joe Hart!
DOESN'T RATE... Bez's hair!

BEZ can usually be found legging it around the country talking to the Premier League superstars – he's actually starting to get pretty good at it!

SUPPORTS... Arsenal
TOP SKILL... Eating pork pies!
RATES... Mesut Ozil!
DOESN'T RATE... Susan Boyle!

MATES WITH THE STARS!

BEZ SAYS: "This is the coolest part of the job. In the last year I've met some of the biggest names in footy. I even flew out to Barcelona to meet Lionel Messi! I asked him for a tour of the city, followed by a meal for two – but he said no. Gutted!"

WORLD CUP VIDEOS!

PAZ SAYS: "I couldn't believe it when the big BBC bosses said they wanted us to make a video diary throughout the World Cup. I had a right laugh ripping all the major gaffes in the Wall of Shame!"

BEZ SAYS: "The best show we did was the one when that football impersonator Darren Farley came on – he's awesome! His Peter Crouch was well funny. If you missed it you can still see it on motdmag.com now!"

> Let's send this to You've Been Framed!

5 OF THE BEST!

BEZ PICKS HIS FAVE FOOTY STARS!

5. FRANK LAMPARD "We swapped stories about how our dads used to shout at us on the touchline when we were in the school team!"

4. ANDREY ARSHAVIN "He cracked me up when he told me not to trust cats because they're like just foxes!"

3. PETER CROUCH "Crouchy told me about how he used to pretend to speak French to confuse the foreign lads at Portsmouth!"

2. THEO WALCOTT "Him and his dad kept trying to put me off when I was recording the show!"

1. DAVID JAMES "He managed to talk for 15 minutes about his hairstyles through the years – he could've gone on for longer!"

> I'm gonna have my hair like Paz!

CHECK IT OUT NOW!

If you still haven't experienced the **MOTD Xtra** buzz, what the flip are you waiting for? Get on **motdmag.com** now and start working your way through all the mint videos and podcasts!

MOTD GAME!
PENALTY$

All you need is a dice, a mate and a pen to play our wicked game!

SHOOT-OUT!

HOW TO PLAY!

1 Get a dice and a mate and you're ready to go – roll the dice and whoever has the highest number goes first!

2 The winner rolls the dice then matches his number up to one on the picture to see if he's scored or missed!

3 Each player gets five rolls and whoever scores the most, wins. Keep count of the score on the scoreboard provided – if it's level after five pens, it's sudden death!

MY SCOREBOARD

Each time you shoot, stick a mark in the box – whoever has the most after five pens, wins!

✓ = Goal   ✗ = Miss

PLAYER 1					PLAYER 2					
PEN 1	PEN 2	PEN 3	PEN 4	PEN 5	PEN 1	PEN 2	PEN 3	PEN 4	PEN 5	ROUND 1
☐	☐	☐	☐	☐	☐	☐	☐	☐	☐	

PLAYER 1					PLAYER 2					
PEN 1	PEN 2	PEN 3	PEN 4	PEN 5	PEN 1	PEN 2	PEN 3	PEN 4	PEN 5	ROUND 2
☐	☐	☐	☐	☐	☐	☐	☐	☐	☐	

PLAYER 1					PLAYER 2					
PEN 1	PEN 2	PEN 3	PEN 4	PEN 5	PEN 1	PEN 2	PEN 3	PEN 4	PEN 5	ROUND 3
☐	☐	☐	☐	☐	☐	☐	☐	☐	☐	

PLAYER 1					PLAYER 2					
PEN 1	PEN 2	PEN 3	PEN 4	PEN 5	PEN 1	PEN 2	PEN 3	PEN 4	PEN 5	ROUND 4
☐	☐	☐	☐	☐	☐	☐	☐	☐	☐	

PLAYER 1					PLAYER 2					
PEN 1	PEN 2	PEN 3	PEN 4	PEN 5	PEN 1	PEN 2	PEN 3	PEN 4	PEN 5	ROUND 5
☐	☐	☐	☐	☐	☐	☐	☐	☐	☐	

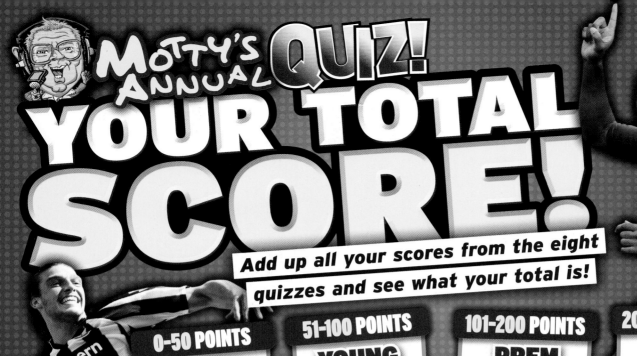

MOTTY'S ANNUAL QUIZ!
YOUR TOTAL SCORE!

Add up all your scores from the eight quizzes and see what your total is!

0-50 POINTS
FREE TRANSFER!
You don't know much about footy, so your club has kicked you out!

51-100 POINTS
YOUNG TALENT!
That's a pretty good quiz score – you've got a big footy future!

101-200 POINTS
PREM HERO!
Cracking score! Your footy brain makes you one of the league's best!

201-250 POINTS
WORLD STAR!
There's only one thing to say after this ace score... you're a legend!

MY TOTAL SCORE IS .... /250

DIEGO MILITO

INTER MILAN & ARGENTINA

WORLD STAR!

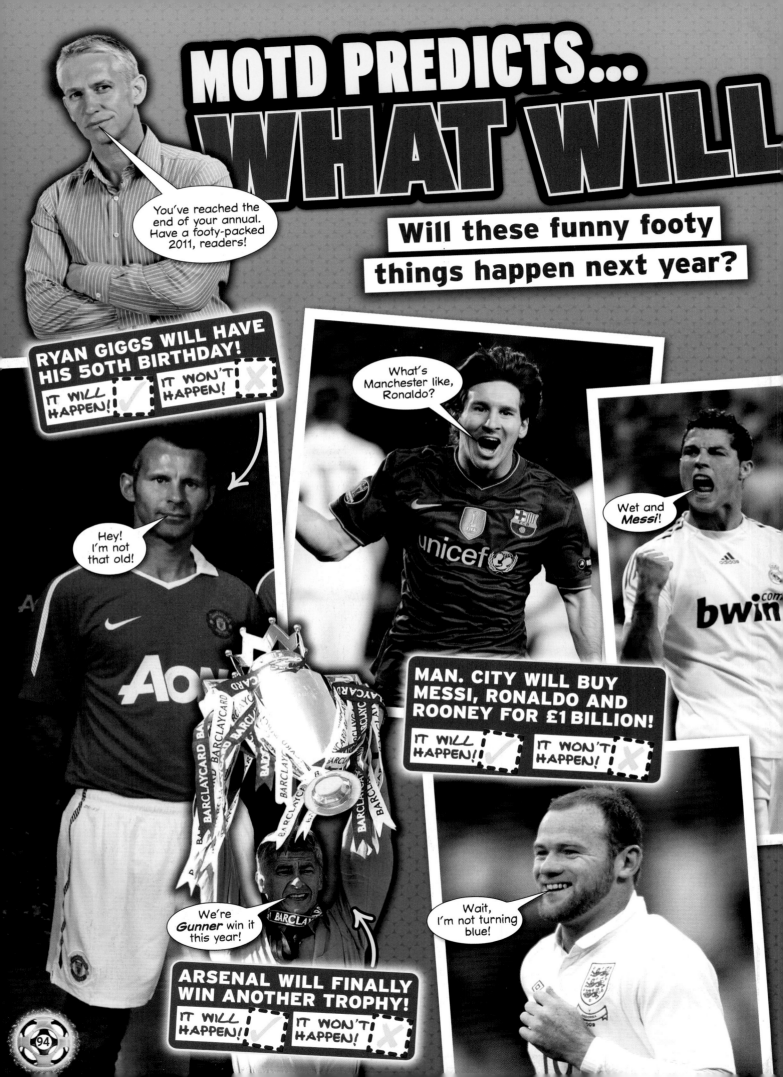